MOTORCYCLE
RIDERS HUB

KEEP IT ON THE BLACK STUFF

MotorcycleRidersHub.co.uk

KEEP IT ON THE BLACK STUFF

ABOUT SIMON HAYES

A full time instructor since 1991, Simon Hayes is a highly experienced motorcycle instructor and well known within the industry. Simon's first six years as an instructor were spent teaching military personnel, where he had a 100% success rate and earned a reputation for high level training.

Since 1996 Simon has operated a respected multisite motorcycle training business covering Birmingham and the Midlands. Over thirty years of dedication to the highest possible standards of motorcycle training has forged a reputation for excellence. Simon has seen many changes and challenges affecting the industry, his own training school has continued to thrive and develop.

Over these decades Simon has covered over a million miles and personally delivered novice to advanced training to many thousands of bikers. Simon is also sought after UK wide as an accomplished instructor trainer and has introduced countless new motorcycle instructors to the sector. In addition, Simon maintains a busy diary of European Tours covering advanced riding on the continent, off road training, track day training, local club and charity rides.

Some years ago, Simon began to improve his students motorcycle training experience through complimentary video based training.

Through pre-course learning students are able to visualise motorcycle skills training and find that their practical training is greatly enhanced.

Over a ten year period, these video training resources were refined, resulting in a first edition being formally published and more widely available.

ABOUT SIMON HAYES CONTINUED...

From starting video training on a DVD, the delivery has been changed and nurtured into Motorcycle Riders Hub, the UK's first 100% video based motorcycle training resource. As the founder of Motorcycle Riders Hub, Simon's vision is to enhance rider training and safety across the UK, empowering both new and experienced riders to continually improve their skills.

Simon believes that the Motorcycle Riders Hub resources should not be used in isolation and must not be viewed as a substitute for professional motorcycle training. To get the best out of the training resource, riders should use the video training and practical training in conjunction to elevate their learning experience. Practical training alone does not give learner riders all the tools they need.

Motorcycle Riders Hub is supported by a number of full time trainers and other professional motorcyclists, as well as an Advisory Panel, they are all committed to road safety and the values of 'Keep it on the black stuff'.

As Motorcycle Riders Hub continues to develop, its aim is to give riders a useful dedicated e-learning platform. Simon's ambition is to reach as many new riders as possible countrywide to help and guide them to become better riders, his commitment to motorcycle training continues with an ongoing full schedule of practical courses.

Motorcycle Riders Hub
Keep it on the black stuff

KEEP IT ON THE BLACK STUFF

ABOUT MOTORCYCLE RIDERS HUB

Over the decades there has been significant changes made to motorcycle training. The latest development in rider training saw the introduction and implementation of CBT, Module 1 and Module 2 motorcycle tests. The result has been a substantial uplift in learner riders skills and ability.

Our vision is to help learner riders at all levels to improve their knowledge, ability and skills by using an online e-learning platform to raise personal riding standards.

Motorcycle Riders Hub is the UK's only 100% online motorcycle video training resource helping learner riders through their Compulsory Basic Training (CBT, Direct Access, Module 1 and Module 2 motorcycle tests.

The online program of dedicated guidance and learning resources will help all riders to develop and enhance their skills, ensuring they are better and safer riders and can keep it on the black stuff.

KEEP IT ON THE BLACK STUFF

CONTENTS

KEEP IT ON THE BLACK STUFF

MOTORCYCLE
RIDERS HUB

LEARNING TO RIDE

Biking is a fabulous pastime, people are learning to ride a motorcycle for economic reasons. On the whole, motorcycles are less expensive to purchase, tax and insure than cars. Taking account of the cost of learning, they offer a cheaper route to getting mobile.

Parking is generally easier and less expensive for motorcycles. It can also mean quicker travel, by allowing riders to minimise the frustrations of traffic congestion. Given these benefits, there is also a good case for motorcycles to be used as a greener mode of transport.

Riders must recognise and take responsibility for their own vulnerability on the roads. This requires an investment in good protective clothing, plus a commitment to both compulsory and ongoing motorcycle training. On today's faster and congested roads, rider responsibility demands the highest levels of observation, anticipation and planning.

Compulsory Basic Training (CBT) is the starting point. It sets the minimum standard for new riders, allowing them to ride unaccompanied on the road, it is effectively the lowest level of rider skill and rider safety. This contentious observation is supported by statistics that attribute most motorcycle accidents to rider error.

For new riders we suggest that Compulsory Basic Training does not tick all the boxes of 'learning to ride a motorcycle'. Novice riders should take to the roads with care, take responsibility and commit to ongoing motorcycle training.

PREPARATION

The Compulsory Basic Training (CBT course was introduced in December 1990. It is a legal requirement for all motorcyclists before they can ride on public roads. Since the introduction of this compulsory training, the UK has seen significant improvements in motorcycle safety and reduced accident statistics.

DRIVING LICENCE REQUIREMENTS

Learner riders must hold a driving licence (full or provisional with the correct category entitlement (A or AM. Those who passed a car test before February 2001, should already have category AM or P entitlement to ride a moped.

A new rider's training experience can be more effective with pre CBT preparations. We recommend the Motorcycle Riders Hub CBT Course, where video and e-learning can boost understanding and knowledge, before undertaking the actual CBT Course.

WHAT TO WEAR

CBT students are required to wear appropriate clothing, as a minimum they must wear a helmet. They should also wear thick denim jeans, a heavy jacket, sturdy boots and motorcycle gloves (if they don't have proper motorcycle clothing. Shorts, T-shirts and trainers are not appropriate.

Having proper motorcycle clothing offers the best protection. Most training schools can loan their students a helmet, gloves and a high viz vest. Some also loan jackets and other items. CBT participants should check well in advance of their training day.

EYE TEST

Glasses and contact lenses are allowed, but before a CBT Course can begin, students are required to read a number plate from 20.5 metres. Poor eyesight commonly goes undiagnosed. If in any doubt an eyesight test is recommended prior to undertaking training.

KEEP IT ON THE BLACK STUFF

MOTORCYCLE
RIDERS HUB

COURSE EXPLAINED

The Motorcycle Riders Hub CBT Course does not substitute professional motorcycle training. It has been structured to enhance the skills and knowledge gained through Compulsory Basic Training (CBT) and as an essential learning platform.

For students embarking on motorcycling for the first time, there is a lot to take in during one days training. This is especially true for those who are completely new to the road who may find it difficult to take it all in and set the required skills.

CBT Course has been put together by a team of highly experienced, skilled and qualified motorcycle instructors. It has been further enhanced through student feedback and then endorsed by an independent Advisory Panel.

Content includes:

▶ Video modules covering essential skills

▶ Instructional training video road rides

▶ Training podcasts

▶ Comprehensive e-book

▶ Tests to measure progress

▶ Motorcycle Instructor top tips

▶ Ongoing updates to the learner resources

The goal of CBT Course is to be a better skilled, more confident and safer rider. The course enhances a student's motorcycle training experience through pre-learning and the opportunity to visualise and internalise the core components of safe motorcycle riding with instructional videos.

To maximise knowledge and understanding, students can watch the videos as many times as they like, plus listen to the podcast, read the e-book and complete the check tests.

The outcome is a better prepared, less stressed training experience. Motorcycle instructors are more empowered to train, because students attend with a higher induction level from home learning prior to them attending the CBT Course.

KEEP IT ON THE BLACK STUFF

RIDER FAULTS

Before completing a CBT, students should be able to ride a two wheeled pushbike. This ensures they have sufficient balance and skill to ride a motorcycle or moped.

CBT students who cannot ride a pushbike (or have not ridden one for some time) will find it difficult riding a motorcycle. Students should refresh their two wheeled skills before attending motorcycle training.

CBT students must have a valid driving licence and any glasses/contact lenses in their possession. This is because training providers are required to check the licence and eyesight of every student. Failing to comply may result in a cancelled CBT and loss of training fee.

During a CBT, new riders need to absorb lots of new information and for this reason, pre CBT study is wise and will result in a better training experience.

The Motorcycle Riders Hub CBT Course is structured to pave the way to the best possible CBT experience.

General advice to avoid a poor CBT experience:

► Avoid feeling rushed, overwhelmed or intimidated

► Opt for training that allows you to learn at your own pace

► Do not look down at the ground when riding

► Don't proceed onto the road ride unless fully confident

► Request more off road training if required

► Study the Highway Code before attending CBT

► Trust Instructor's judgement, listen and take their advice

► Accept that it is natural to feel a little apprehensive at first

► Always be safe, in control of both emotions and motorcycle

x

OBSERVATIONS

Novice riders must learn to shift their attention from their motorcycle controls and the road just ahead of their front wheel, to what is happening ahead, behind and to the sides. They must develop the skills to adjust position for the best view, have good observations and react accordingly to what they see.

Rear checks - are required before signalling, changing direction, altering speed and on approach to hazards. They involve turning the head to look behind into the motorcyclists blind spot, along with the effective use of mirrors. blind spots are the areas to the sides and slightly to the rear that are not visible through the mirrors.

Rear observations ensure full awareness and allow riders to ensure that it is safe to continue with their plan. They also inform other road users of an intended manoeuvre. Rear checks are required when indicating, slowing down or stopping, changing lanes, overtaking, moving off and negotiating junctions.

New riders must develop the skill of correctly timing their rear observations and recognise when such observations might be dangerous. They should also avoid getting into the bad habit of looking over the shoulder too frequently or at the wrong time.

During rear observations, riders can momentarily lose touch with what is happening ahead, plus run the risk of veering off course. In heavy traffic, whilst travelling at speed or when overtaking, poorly timed or excessive rear observations can be dangerous.

Novice riders must also understand and learn that in certain situations, failing to use effective rear observations can be dangerous. Examples include, when turning right into minor roads, when moving out to overtake a slower moving vehicle.

Lifesaver checks - are the final shoulder observations to the left or right blind spot area before committing to a manoeuvre. When performing lifesavers, new riders must take care not to adversely affect their motorcycles balance or steering which may alter their road position.

MIRRORS - OBSERVATIONS - LIFESAVERS

KEEP IT ON THE BLACK STUFF

OBSERVATIONS CONTINUED...

Forward observations - are as critical as rearward observations and new riders must develop the ability to constantly interpret what is happening ahead. As well as looking directly in front, observations are extended to the middle and far distance, as well as implementing good forward scanning techniques.

Skilled riders will constantly use extended forward vision and observations, using them to adjust speed and stop safely if necessary. Effective forward observations aids effective awareness and planning, with the scope to respond to the changing environment and developing hazards.

Parked vehicles, road furniture, hedgerows and other obstructions can block a rider's view. Skilled riders use good vision to anticipate, decide on a plan and safely adapt a new riding position to maximise their view.

Riders must extend their observations to anticipate the actions of other road users and then position to be seen and give more room for error. This is especially important when approaching junctions where other vehicles are waiting to emerge and may not have seen an approaching motorcyclist.

In moving traffic, riders must be aware of other vehicles blind spots. The use of high visibility motorcycle clothing and the use of dipped headlights, even in daytime riding is advised.

Effective observation also includes using clues to anticipate potential hazards. For instance, for vehicles parked outside a school, there might be a risk of children suddenly running out, or car doors opening or vehicles suddenly pulling away.

Developing good observation is essential to increasing rider safety. The key to improving these and other skills relies on rider responsibility and recognising the importance of ongoing professional motorcycle training. With this commitment to training comes higher levels of competency, increased safety, greater confidence and a vastly enhanced riding experience.

KEEP IT ON THE BLACK STUFF

MOTORCYCLE
RIDERS HUB

THE 5 BASIC CONTROLS

There are five basic controls that must be mastered in order to safely operate and ride a motorcycle. There are many other important controls, but until a new rider has reached a level of proficiency with these five basic controls, they will struggle with other aspects of riding a motorcycle.

Overview:

Clutch

- ▶ Disengages the drive when in gear
- ▶ Pull in the clutch to select first gear
- ▶ Use it slowly when pulling away
- ▶ Vital for slow control and stopping
- ▶ Aids smoother gear changes

Throttle

- ▶ Use a flat wrist
- ▶ Use gently, do not be aggressive
- ▶ Turn it away from rider to allow engine braking

Front brake

- ▶ All four fingers
- ▶ Finger tips only
- ▶ When the bike is in an upright position and in a straight line
- ▶ From high speed to low speed
- ▶ Never in a corner or when bike is leaned over
- ▶ Not used at slow speeds or when steering the handlebars

Rear brake

- ▶ Only at slow speed
- ▶ Use when cornering or steering the handlebars

Gear lever

- ▶ Sequential gearbox - up or down one gear at a time
- ▶ Speed up - change up
- ▶ Slow down - change down

HOW TO HOLD THE BARS

Having the correct grip on the handlebars is imperative when riding a motorcycle. By adopting a light grip, learner riders will avoid suffering with sore hands, tension in the arms, shoulders and neck.

A light grip translates to being more relaxed and less fatigued, along with improved handling skills.

Right hand

The right hand operates the throttle. Maintaining a flat wrist posture, without angling the wrist over or dropping it down will result in a far more effective operation of the throttle. This ensures maximum control, without getting a sore wrist. The thumb of the right hand should be used to operate the right-handlebar switchgear, whilst ensuring a full grip remains on the throttle. Fingertips should be used to operate the front brake.

Left hand

The left hand holds the left-handlebar grip and when needed the fingertips are used to operate the clutch. The thumb of the left hand is used to operate the left handlebar switchgear.

Instructor Tips

"Remember the grip on the bars should be enough to have full control, just a 'light but secure grip' will suffice."

"If experiencing tension in the shoulders - relax the shoulders and wiggle the fingers. This eases tension, the elbows will drop and shoulders will become more relaxed."

KEEP IT ON THE BLACK STUFF

MOTORCYCLE
RIDERS HUB

OPERATING THE CONTROLS

With respect to these additional controls, it is natural for learner riders to glance down to use them initially. Practice is the essential stepping stone to a rider keeping their eyes on the road, whilst operating the other controls. Even though motorcycle controls can vary slightly between models, the most common configuration is as follows:

Left switch gear

Controls that are operated with the thumb of the left hand are:

▶ Horn

▶ Left and right indicator switch

▶ Indicator cancelling switch

▶ Headlight (low and high beam).

▶ The passing light switch is normally situated on the front of the left switch gear and is operated using the first finger of the left hand.

Central controls

There may be some variations on different motorcycles, for most learner style motorcycles, the only central control is the ignition. This can be operated with either hand and would only be operated whilst the motorcycle is stationary and out of gear (in neutral).

▶ Clocks

▶ Speedometer

▶ Rev counter

▶ Fuel gauge

▶ Indicator and warning lights

Right switch gear

Controls that are operated with the thumb of the right hand are:

▶ Starter button

▶ Emergency kill switch.

Instructor Tip

"There are of additional accessory switches, such as heated grips, that can be fitted for rider comfort."

KEEP IT ON THE BLACK STUFF

DAILY MOTORCYCLE CHECKS - VOLTS

Riders should learn how to check their motorcycle on a daily basis. Basic daily checks should only take a minute, so there is no excuse!

Confidence in a motorcycle's road worthiness increases rider safety.

If higher mileage journeys are being planned, then more extensive checks are required. In relation to basic daily checks, see below:

Daily checks (VOLTS)

This is a useful mnemonic to remember the essential daily checks must be carried out at the beginning of each day or journey.

V - Visual

O - Oil

L - Lights

T - Tyres and brakes

S - Steering and suspension

There are a number of commonly used mnemonics used to reference daily motorcycle checks, VOLTS being a popular one. Learner riders are advised to check with their local training provider, who may have a good alternative.

Instructor Tips

"Ensure you check the owners handbook on how to check your bike. You should make time to check the tyres air, condition and tread."

"Mnemonics are a memory word that helps learners recall larger pieces of information, in this case in the form of a list of words to help you remember what to check."

BASIC MOTORCYCLE CHECKS - POWDDERSSS

Riders should learn how to fully check their motorcycle to ensure that it is roadworthy at all times. The road is dangerous enough without adding further risk by not having a serviceable motorcycle.

Weekly Motorcycle checks - POWDDERSSS

Instructors always offer advice on how to keep a motorcycle in a safe and roadworthy condition. To help remember the essential weekly checks, the mnemonic POWDDERSSS is a good memory aid.

There are a number of other excellent approaches to use the right routine for weekly checks. Learner riders are advised to check with their local training school for their trainers' preferred method.

P - Petrol

O - Oil

W - Water

D - Drive

D - Damage

E - Electric

R - Rubber

S - Steering

S - Suspension

S - Stopping

It is also important to refer to the owner's manual for specific checks and servicing requirements.

Instructor Tips

"The chain should be checked at its tightest point (ask your trainer for more information) and ensure the oil / chain lube does not go onto the rear tyre."

"When checking the dipstick, remove, wipe clean, reinsert (do not screw back in), take out and check the level."

KEEP IT ON THE BLACK STUFF

SAFETY POSITION

The safety position:

(1) sitting on the motorcycle

(2) right foot on the rear brake

(3) both hands holding the handlebars

(4) head up, looking forward to
   aid stability and balance

(5) left foot supporting the motorcycle,
   first gear must be selected
   (with the clutch in), ready to pull away

Adopting the safety position aids full throttle control whilst pulling away. If the front brake is applied, it would be difficult to pull away being in full control of the throttle.

By having the right foot up and on the rear brake

► correct brake is applied

► rear brake light is illuminated

► bike will not roll on a hill

► right foot is out of harm's way

► less danger in the event of a nudge from the rear

The safety position is an essential skill that all learner riders should master. As a riding discipline, using the safety position early in training, will result in a novice rider learning how to sit correctly from the start.

Mastering the safety position helps with a number of manoeuvres e.g. hill starts and angle start.

KEEP IT ON THE BLACK STUFF

MOTORCYCLE
RIDERS HUB

SELECTING 1st GEAR AND NEUTRAL

An essential step to getting a motorcycle moving is being confident in selecting both first gear and neutral. This skill requires the learner rider to understand how the clutch is operated in conjunction with the gears and the relationship between the clutch, the gears and the throttle.

Before moving away for the first time, riders should practice the process of pulling' the clutch lever in, to engage both first gear and neutral. They should also learn what to do if second gear is inadvertently selected if trying to select neutral.

Selecting first gear from neutral

▶ Apply front brake and put right foot on floor

▶ Pull in the clutch and left foot onto the foot peg

▶ Left toe pushes down onto the gear lever and select 1st gear

▶ Left foot down, lift the right foot up and apply the rear brake

▶ Release the front brake and hold the throttle correctly

Selecting neutral from first gear

▶ Apply front brake and right foot down

▶ Lift the left foot and push the gear lever up into neutral

▶ Left foot down and apply the rear brake with the right foot

▶ Release the clutch lever with both brakes still applied

▶ Release the front brake lever and hold throttle correctly

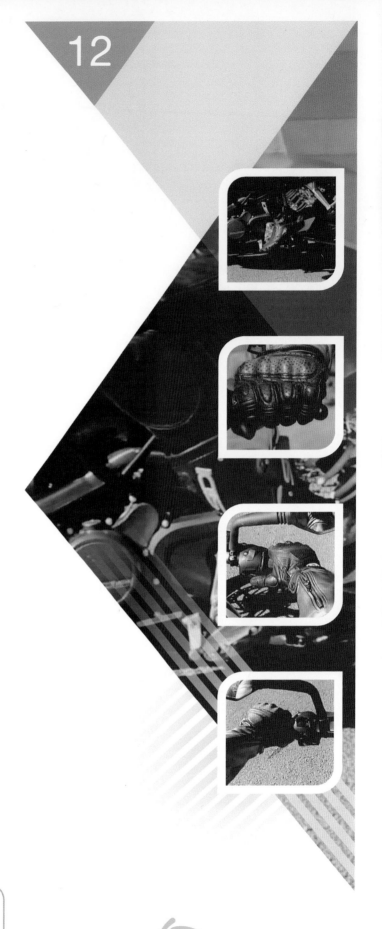

Instructor Tip

"If the bike stalls, pull in the clutch and start the motorcycle in first gear."

KEEP IT ON THE BLACK STUFF

MOTORCYCLE
RIDERS HUB

PULLING AWAY AND STOPPING

The process of learning to pull away and stop for the first time is exciting. It is at this point that the five main motorcycle controls are used. Riders will use the throttle, clutch, front brake, rear brake and gears.

This aspect of learning to ride a motorcycle takes a significant amount of time and should not be rushed. Motorcycle instructors will nurture and skilfully guide their students step by step, until novice riders become competent with this skill to move on to the next stage of training.

Learner riders should to be patient, take their time and accept that repetition is the key to success. Improving riding skills demands a step by step approach and when learning to pull away and stop, the objective is to gain confidence in coordinating the basic motorcycle controls.

Throttle - use a flat wrist and only a small amount of revs to get the motorcycle moving forwards.

Clutch - use the ends of the fingers only to use the clutch bite. Make sure the clutch control is smooth and get used to using a sustained biting point, this can feel unnatural at first.

Front brake - there is no requirement to use the front brake whilst pulling away and stopping at slow speed. If the front brake is used in error, ensure the bike is travelling in a straight line. If both feet are on the ground to aid stability the rider will have to use the front brake. If the front brake is used it should be used gently and never aggressively.

Rear brake - this is the recommended brake to use for all slow control exercises.

Gear lever - having mastered selecting first gear and neutral, pulling away and stopping builds confidence and skills when introducing the other controls.

KEEP IT ON THE BLACK STUFF

MOTORCYCLE
RIDERS HUB

SLOW CONTROL

Slow control skills are essential to road safety and come into play in a wide variety of situations. Slow moving or queued traffic, slow control is required by using the clutch, throttle, gears and rear brake.

Also when approaching and negotiating road junctions. Other situations where slow control is required includes: filtering, riding in congestion, riding/pulling away on an incline, riding in car parks and in any situation where safety dictates.

This skill requires novice riders to become confident in controlling the speed and forward movement of the motorcycle by feathering the clutch to maintain biting point. This requires fine clutch control, where the clutch is held between being engaged and disengaged. The throttle is maintained with more revs required, to give sufficient power to the engine to prevent it from stalling. The rear brake can be used to slow the speed of the bike when required.

Slow control riding is usually at walking speed and generally around 3-4 mph. Any slower than this and novice riders will experience balance issues. Any faster and the rider will be relying on the throttle to control the speed of the bike instead of using the correct balance of clutch and throttle.

Use the following to aid slow control:

Clutch - on the clutch bite to control the speed

Throttle - to stop the engine from stalling

Rear brake - to slow the bike if travelling too fast

Left foot - only needed to engage first gear to pull away

Head position - looking up for balance and stability

Front brake - do not use when moving slowly

KEEP IT ON THE BLACK STUFF

MOTORCYCLE
RIDERS HUB

FIGURE-OF-EIGHT

The figure of-eight is a slow control exercise. It brings together the co-ordination of clutch, throttle and rear brake, along with the introduction of steering and the correct riding posture.

For learner riders the figure-of-eight is not an easy manoeuvre to master. Head position becomes vital, with a requirement to keep the head up and looking in the direction of travel. The exercise also gives riders the opportunity to practice maintaining effective throttle and clutch control whilst steering the bike to the left and right.

A good technique is to imagine a centre point between the two cones and to use this imagined point as an aiming marker for each complete turn. The rider should arrive back to the same centre point each time in preparation to ride the next 'circle'.

Circles can be large to start with and even in shape to make this exercise easier, making them smaller the more proficient they become.

Remember:

▶ Keep the head up to aid balance and stability

▶ Be gentle with the throttle

▶ Clutch at biting point at all times to control the bikes speed

▶ Rear brake only during this exercise

▶ Look where you want the bike to go

▶ Keep the chin up

▶ Steer the bike smoothly when turning

Instructor Tip

"Do not use the front brake whilst steering during each circle / circuit."

KEEP IT ON THE BLACK STUFF

MOTORCYCLE
RIDERS HUB

U-TURN

The U-turn exercise is a great opportunity for new riders to practice developing their slow control skills a confined area. Confidence in this manoeuvre is important in real life road situations between kerbs.

This U-turn is usually practised in a safe environment between painted lines or a set of cones. This ensures there are no physical barriers in place in the early stages. The U-turn exercise requires control of the clutch, throttle, rear brake, steering, posture and head position.

The key is for the rider to create maximum room within the turning area, whilst maintaining full control of the clutch, throttle and rear brake (if needed).

Mirror checks and lifesavers are required, as this exercise is intended to represent riding a U-turn between two kerbs on the road. There is a safety need for good observations and a lifesaver before turning.

Remember:

▶ Carry out rear observations before pulling away

▶ Keep the machine steady and under full control whilst riding parallel to the line (kerb)

▶ Carry out a lifesaver before turning

▶ Ensure motorcycle is close to the line (kerb) prior to turning, this creates a maximum turning area

▶ Look in the intended direction of travel throughout

▶ Make good steering movement and commit to the turn

Instructor Tip

"Don't worry if it seems difficult to start with, practice makes perfect."

KEEP IT ON THE BLACK STUFF

CHANGING GEAR

Operating the gears and ensuring that the correct gear is selected is an important skill to master. As well as being aware of how gears should be matched to the bikes speed, it is also important to understand how gears are selected in relation to the motorcycle speed in all conditions.

Key point to remember

- ▶ Speed-up   :   change-up
- ▶ Slow-down   :   change-down

During training, learner riders will learn about the motorcycle's sequential gear box and how to use the controls to smoothly to change gear.

Changing up

- ▶ Throttle off before each gear change

- ▶ Clutch in and select the next highest gear

- ▶ Don't rush the gear change

- ▶ Release the gear lever fully

- ▶ Release the clutch before using the throttle

Changing down

- ▶ Throttle off before each gear change

- ▶ Brake to bring the bike to the desired speed

- ▶ Clutch in and select the next lowest gear

- ▶ Release the clutch slowly to take up the drive

- ▶ At desired speed release the brakes and continue riding

Instructor Tip

"Push the gear lever firmly. It will only select one gear higher or lower on each single press."

KEEP IT ON THE BLACK STUFF

MOTORCYCLE
RIDERS HUB

CONTROLLED BRAKING

The front brake is the more powerful brake and must be used gently. For an effective application of the brake, learner riders should use all four fingers and avoid snatching or grabbing the brake lever. The front brake should only be used when the bike is in an upright position and travelling in a straight line. It must not be used in a corner.

The rear brake is less effective at higher speeds. At speed, it is generally used in conjunction with the front brake. However, if needing to slow down in a bend, the rear brake would be used on its own. As a general rule, use the rear brake on its own when riding slowly or turning the handlebars.

Both brakes

▶ Used together from high speed to low speed

▶ When the bike is in an upright position

▶ Travelling in a straight line

Front brake only

▶ Sometimes taught as a means of giving a signal to the traffic behind when taking off a small amount of speed.

▶ Generally, the front brake is not used on its own to slow down or stop

Rear brake only

▶ Slow control situations

▶ When steering the bike

▶ In a bend or corner

Engine braking

▶ At the start of every slowing down manoeuvre

▶ In a corner

▶ Losing a few miles per hour

▶ When it won't affect any road users behind

KEEP IT ON THE BLACK STUFF

MOTORCYCLE
RIDERS HUB

EMERGENCY STOP

An emergency stop should be a last resort, good forward planning should prevent the need for an emergency stop. It is far better to identify hazards early enough so that a rider never has the need to carry out a quick braking exercise.

In the event that emergency braking is required, riders should stay upright and travel in a straight line. Some motorcycles have ABS (Anti-lock Braking Systems), but if motorcycles don't have it and the wheel's lock, release the brakes immediately to regain traction and then re-apply them with less pressure.

Dry conditions

▶ Throttle off

▶ Apply front brake to allow the brakes to start binding

▶ Apply rear brake a fraction of a second later

▶ Gentle application of both brakes

▶ Continue to squeeze the front brake only

▶ Keep the brakes applied until the bike stops

▶ Just before stopping, pull the clutch in to prevent the bike stalling

▶ No gear changes are necessary until stopped

▶ Put left foot down to stabilise the bike

Wet conditions

▶ Throttle off

▶ Apply front brake to allow the brakes to start binding

▶ Apply rear brake a fraction of a second later

▶ Gentle application of both brakes

▶ Continue to squeeze evenly on both brakes

▶ Keep the brakes applied until the bike stops

▶ Just before stopping, pull the clutch in to prevent the bike stalling

▶ No gear changes are necessary until stopped

▶ Put left foot down to stabilise the bike

KEEP IT ON THE BLACK STUFF

MOTORCYCLE
RIDERS HUB

BASIC COUNTER STEERING

Counter steering is an essential skill to safely negotiate bends and corners. At slow speed the handlebars are turned to steer the bike (as with the U-turn and figure-of eight). Counter steering takes time to master and learner riders tend to improve as they develop through practice.

Riders should ensure that their speed in corners does not exceed their ability.

Simple explanation (push on the inside bar)

▶ To steer right - Look right - Push right
▶ To steer left   - Look left   - Push left

Look in the direction of intended travel. In a bend look through the corner and to the exit of the bend. Locate the aiming point through the corner and at the start of the corner, gently push the handlebar with the palm of the hand down and away from the body (in the direction of travel). This weight transfer results in the motorcycle leaning in to the corner and as this happens, it becomes a natural manoeuvre to negotiate the bend.

Counter steering is a skill and must be understood, practiced and mastered. With practice comes confidence, and the ability to put the motorcycle where the rider wants to end up.

Remember:

▶ Look in the direction of travel

▶ Keep the head up, look ahead and through the corner

▶ Do not look down at the ground in front of the bike

▶ Do not focus on a single point

▶ With the palm of the hand, push the handlebar forward, down and in the intended direction of travel

▶ Relax and go with it

▶ Lean slightly in to the corner if necessary

KEEP IT ON THE BLACK STUFF

NEGOTIATING JUNCTIONS - OSMPSL

The **OSMPSL** routine is the DVSA recognised system of riding, it was designed to help learner riders approach junctions, roundabouts and other hazards.

For learner riders, **OSMPSL** acts as a perfect starting point, helping them to develop good riding habits and to make safe decisions. The **OSMPSL** routine offers an excellent foundation, but must be adjusted when necessary.

As novice riders improve their skills, experience and confidence, the **OSMPSL** routine can be adjusted for the prevailing conditions and scenarios .

O - Observation: Check all around, into the blind spot and behind and gather information in the riders vicinity.

S - Signal: Given in plenty of time to warn others of the intended manoeuvre. Avoid giving false indications or indicating too early.

M - Manoeuvre: Carry out the appropriate observations (mirror checks and lifesavers) and manoeuvre the motorcycle.

P - Position: Adopt the correct road position when approaching a junction or hazard. Be aware of road surface hazards before moving.

S - Speed: Reduce speed in good time using a combination of engine braking, front and rear brakes. Be prepared to stop at junctions.

L - Look: Approaching the junction or hazard look into the intended area of travel and ensure it is safe to proceed. Carry out further observations and a lifesaver if necessary.

KEEP IT ON THE BLACK STUFF

POOR JUNCTION CONTROL

Early preparation on approach to junctions and hazards are vital. With regards to braking and gear changes, riders should aim to be in the correct position, at the correct speed and in the correct gear at all times. This takes practice to perfect and learner riders are advised to keep the speed down, allowing more thinking time. This results in safer decisions and less anxiety.

On approach close the throttle to take advantage of engine braking. From high speeds, apply both brakes to slow down and to show a brake light to the vehicles behind. During this braking phase, change down the gears one at a time to help reduce speed.

At about 15 mph, the motorcycle should be in second gear. When around 2-3 car lengths from the junction or hazard, transfer to the rear brake only. This method of approach keeps the motorcycle stable, with maximum control, ensuring the rider is at the correct speed to make a good decision to either stop or go.

Remember:

▶ Throttle off when slowing down

▶ Use engine braking to help reduce speed

▶ Use both brakes from high to low speed

▶ If a vehicle is behind, show a brake light

▶ Release front brake and transfer to rear brake only for slow speed control when close to the junction or hazard

▶ Do not use the front brake in a bend or if steering the handlebars

▶ Being prepared gives more time to make good, safe decisions

SLOWING DOWN FOR JUNCTIONS

Avoid looking late into junctions as this can cause a late decision to stop, along with overloaded front suspension and affecting balance. A rider is unlikely to be in the best position to safely exit the junction if they look late into the junction. This can result in a rider steering wide and even veering on to the wrong side of the road, which can be very dangerous.

Another risk associated with looking late and poor position is dropping the motorcycle.

By looking early, a good decision can be made, allowing the rider to look in the direction of travel, position the bike correctly and exit the junction safely.

A proper junction approach, with early observations will allow the rider to follow the kerb (if turning left) and if there is a need to stop, the riders position is good for moving forward again in the correct direction.

Remember:

▶ Slow down early and always be ready to stop

▶ Make a decision one car length from the junction

▶ Look forward and stop, or look forward to go

▶ Don't take extra glances after the decision has been made, this will affect road position

▶ Take sufficient time and do not rush

Instructor Tip

"Slow down early on approach to the junction, to ensure the rider is always prepared to stop."

T JUNCTION - TURN LEFT

(LEFT TURN: MINOR TO MAJOR)

The most common junctions for learner riders to negotiate are T junctions and side roads.

In all cases the OSMPSL routine is the key to preparation when approaching a junction. Riders should slow down in plenty of time and look early into the junction, ensuring the best road position is adopted, ready to stop or continue.

Turning left at a T junction (also known as left turn, minor to major), is one of the easiest junctions but it does have a few risk factors to consider.

On approach, riders will normally need to position slightly left in the left wheel track (where the left hand wheel of a car would generally be), but be aware of road surface hazards and parked vehicles.

Be vigilant and look out for overtaking traffic by using mirror checks as required. Once at the junction be aware of impatient road users trying to overtake.

Remember:

▶ Also known as a 'left turn - minor to major'

▶ Use the OSMPSL routine on approach

▶ Ensure position is correct and protect road space

▶ Adopt the correct speed on approach

▶ Always be ready to stop at the junction

▶ Decide a car length away from the junction to either look forward and stop in first gear behind the white line. Or to look forward, in the direction of travel and ride on

▶ Follow the kerb line around at the junction for good position

▶ When safe, go out of the junction slowly and under control

Instructor Tip

"Cancel signal, once in the new lane."

KEEP IT ON THE BLACK STUFF

MOTORCYCLE
RIDERS HUB

T JUNCTION - TURN RIGHT
(RIGHT TURN: MINOR TO MAJOR)

Turning right at a T junction will require using the OSMPSL routine, slow down early enough to look into the junction in both directions. Turning right at a T junction is considered one of the hardest junctions for a learner rider to negotiate. Approach, positioning and slow control are key, as this particular junction requires the rider to give way in both directions.

Time spent in the safety of an off road training area, practising slow control and confidently pulling away are key to success.

Always be ready to stop (unless there is a mandatory stop sign), approaching this junction at the correct speed, in the correct gear and with best positioning will allow a decision to be made by looking into the junction early.

There is still a requirement to maintain rearward observations, in case of other road users trying to undertake or overtake. Other hazards to be aware of include: drain covers, road surface, parked vehicles and oncoming traffic.

Remember:

▶ Also known as a 'turning right - minor to major'

▶ OSMPSL routine is key to success

▶ Position correctly on approach to protect road space

▶ Adopt the correct speed on approach to position, look and decide

▶ Always be prepared to stop at the junction

▶ Decide a car length from the junction to 1) look forward and stop 2) in first gear 3) behind the white line. Or look forward in the direction of travel and ride forward

▶ Aim slightly to the right at the mouth of the junction

▶ When safe, ride on slowly, under control and safely

KEEP IT ON THE BLACK STUFF

MOTORCYCLE
RIDERS HUB

SIDE ROAD - TURN LEFT
(LEFT TURN: MAJOR TO MINOR)

Left turns tend to be easier, especially for learner riders. It is important to use the OSMPSL routine, reduce speed in plenty of time and ensure the correct road position and look early to assess the junction.

When approaching this kind of junction, riders can position slightly left, in the left wheel track (where the left hand wheels of a car are normally positioned). Be aware of road surface and other hazards i.e. drain covers, leaves, loose gravel and parked vehicles. Maintain good rearward observations, being aware of possible overtaking traffic, as other vehicles may be impatient.

An alternative position is to stay in the centre of the lane and to dominate the road on approach. Local motorcycle training providers will have their own views on correct junction position and their advice should be sought.

Remember:

► Also known as 'left turn, major to minor'

► Use the OSMPSL routine on approach

► Ensure correct position and protect road space

► Adopt the correct speed on approach

► Follow the kerb line around at the junction for good position

► Do not accelerate too early and avoid drifting wide

Instructor Tip

"Cancel signal, once in the new lane."

SIDE ROAD - TURN RIGHT
(RIGHT TURN: MAJOR TO MINOR)

Turning right into a side road (also referred to as 'right turn, major to minor') is often a difficult turn for learner riders. This is because of the required position, to the right of the lane, close to the centre of the road. Plus, there is the complication of giving way to oncoming traffic, along with the need for rear observations to be aware of impatient road users who may try to overtake or undertake.

As with all junctions, the OSMPSL routine must be used, along with slow speed control to allow time to look early into the junction.

Riders must ensure they are in the correct gear, at the correct speed and in the correct position. If it is clear do a lifesaver around two car lengths from the turn. This gives time to look forward and assess the road ahead, at this stage there is still enough time to either turn safely or to stop. Where the decision is to stop, another lifesaver is necessary before turning.

Remember:

► Also known as 'right turn, major to minor'

► Use the OSMPSL routine

► Ensure correct position on approach to protect road space

► Adopt the correct speed on approach

► Always be prepared to stop at the junction

► Lifesaver before committing to right turn

► Ride slowly and do not rush

► Avoid cutting the corner or turning late and 'swan-necking'

► When safe, make the turn under control and adopt the correct position

Nb. Check with local motorcycle trainer for definition of 'swan-necking' and the problems that can arise

KEEP IT ON THE BLACK STUFF

 MOTORCYCLE
RIDERS HUB

ROUNDABOUTS - TURN LEFT

Learner riders will need to negotiate a variety of roundabouts. The most common roundabout will have four spokes, with four individual junctions. The OSMPSL routine is an important process when approaching roundabouts. Riders must adopt an appropriate speed, correct gear and move in to the correct road position. They must also look into the roundabout to assess traffic flow.

Turning left at a roundabout is very similar to turning left at a T-junction. A key difference is the need to maintain a central and dominant position in the chosen lane on approach. This is to prevent vehicles behind squeezing past in the same lane.

If the roundabout is clear on approach and it is safe, look forward and in the intended direction of travel. Ride into the roundabout, stay in the centre of the left hand lane and safely leave the roundabout at the first exit. Cancel signal in the new lane before accelerating away.

Remember:

▶ Use the OSMPSL routine on approach

▶ Ensure correct road position to protect road space

▶ Adopt correct speed on approach

▶ Always approach with the intention to stop

▶ Stop if there is any doubt or unsure

▶ Take enough time, do not be pressured and do not rush

▶ Remain in the centre of left hand lane

ROUNDABOUTS - STRAIGHT AHEAD

As with all junctions, correctly using the OSMPSL routine is important. Riders should approach the roundabout at an appropriate speed, in the correct gear, adopt a dominant position and be in the centre of their lane.

Take note of any road markings and if there aren't any, use the left hand lane. The approach is exactly the same as for turning left, but without the need to indicate, which shows the intention to ride straight ahead.

Time must be taken to look early into the roundabout and once the decision to go is made, move into the centre of the left hand lane (also referred to as the outer lane).

On reaching the point of no return (in line with the exit before the one to be taken), indicator left to leave the roundabout. Carry out a lifesaver to ensure it is safe to leave the roundabout and then exit into the new lane. Once in the new lane cancel the signal.

Professional motorcycle training is imperative, especially for complicated roundabouts. A local training provider will ensure riders know how to deal with various roundabouts safely before being unaccompanied on the road.

Remember:

► Use the OSMPSL routine on approach

► Ensure correct position to protect road space

► Adapt to the correct speed on approach

► Always be prepared to stop at the roundabout

► Stay in the middle of the outer (left hand) lane for safety

► Take sufficient time and do not rush

► In the roundabout, avoid cutting across into the inner lane

► Lifesaver or observation before leaving the roundabout

KEEP IT ON THE BLACK STUFF

MOTORCYCLE
RIDERS HUB

ROUNDABOUTS - TURN RIGHT

The OSMPSL routine is vital when approaching a busy roundabout. Riders must take notice of road markings and if there aren't any, use the right hand lane. Indicate right and move into the middle of the right hand lane on approach. Maintaining a dominant lane position prevents other vehicles from squeezing past in the same lane.

Approach the roundabout at an appropriate speed, select the correct gear and in the middle of the lane. Look early into the roundabout, assess the traffic flow and make a decision to ride on or stop.

Once a decision to go is made, move into the centre of the right hand lane (also referred to as the inner lane). It may be necessary to take a lifesaver to the left on entering the roundabout (as a safety check). Do not cut across the left lane.

Once in position in the right hand lane, continue to look in the intended direction of travel and on reaching the point of no return, change signal to the left and carry out a left lifesaver to exit the roundabout. Once in the new lane cancel signal. This can be challenging for learner/novice riders so professional training is essential.

Remember:

▶ Use the OSMPSL routine on approach

▶ Ensure correct position to protect road space

▶ Adopt the correct speed on approach

▶ Always be prepared to stop at the roundabout

▶ Stay in the middle of the inner (right hand) lane

▶ Do not drift across into the left lane, whilst going around the roundabout

▶ Swap signal from right to left at the point of no return

▶ Lifesaver to the left before exiting the roundabout

▶ If after signalling and carrying out a lifesaver, it isn't clear to exit, go around again and repeat the sequence to exit

KEEP IT ON THE BLACK STUFF

URBAN ROAD RIDING

Although not as intense as riding in the city, urban riding is still a risk for novice riders. With more than half of all motorcycle casualties occurring on urban roads, statistics show that new riders must be careful when they first take to the road.

More than half the casualties involve a collision with a car, where the most common factors are **failed to look properly** or **poor turn or manoeuvre**. These incidents most commonly occur at road junctions with crossroads, staggered junctions and roundabouts being the highest risk and where accidents are associated with riders going straight ahead.

Urban riding conditions can vary dramatically at different times of the day, with the heaviest traffic occurring early morning, late afternoon during rush hour and mid afternoon school runs. At these times, car drivers become oblivious as they go about their business, with ineffective observations and motorcycle riders become increasingly invisible.

Poor driver observations are worsened by vehicle blind spots and a multitude of street furniture that can obscure a driver's view. Riders must always have their wits about them and should wear high visibility clothing to be seen.

Riders on mopeds have the added vulnerability of their speed being restricted to 30mph. Virtually all other traffic is capable of higher speeds, L plates are sometimes viewed as a hindrance to impatient car drivers who will try to overtake as soon as possible. This also applies to all riders who display L Plates.

Motorcyclists account for less than 1% of road traffic but 25% of KSI (Killed or Seriously Injured). Risk is better managed by riders taking responsibility, adopting defensive riding skills and continuing with further motorcycle training.

Statistics show that young and inexperienced riders are more vulnerable, they require further coaching for handling skills, road position, planning and awareness. Ignorance and blaming other road users and not taking responsibility are not good excuses and offer no protection.

KEEP IT ON THE BLACK STUFF

MOTORCYCLE
RIDERS HUB

CITY CENTRE RIDING

City riding, with its heavy and congested traffic, can be challenging with more risks to be aware of. Car drivers are in their own bubble and fail to see motorcycles. During the morning rush-hour, commuters can be half asleep and during the winter months many fail to clean their car windows properly. People driving in vehicles often have other distractions, such as mobile phones, music, passengers and even just daydreaming on auto-pilot.

Riders become invisible in these circumstances and when blind spots on cars, buses and trucks are factored in, it is easy to understand why motorcycle riders are more vulnerable. Rider responsibility and defensive riding play a crucial role in managing risk. After completing the CBT, riders are strongly advised to take further training.

For car drivers, road congestion can make their journey, time consuming and frustrating. Car drivers are more inclined to challenge for position, get road rage and become annoyed because they are always stuck in traffic.

Motorcyclists must be aware of this and not become part of the problem. They must remain calm, focused, aware and should ride slowly through traffic, taking advantage of situations where they can filter safely.

Riders also need to consider their bike's performance in the city. In a 30mph speed limit, a 50cc machine should have sufficient speed to keep up with the flow of traffic but on a 40mph road, it may struggle to keep up and the rider may be more vulnerable. In such situations, good forward observation and planning are essential to avoid incidents. Riders must adopt a defensive riding style on every journey and are strongly advised to take further motorcycle training to enhance their city riding skills.

Riding a motorcycle in heavy traffic and congestion is not easy. Luck has no part to play and riders who take chances are at a much higher risk and will add to accident statistics that continue to rise.

MOTORCYCLE
RIDERS HUB

RURAL RIDING

Rural riding can have a variety of risks when you factor in the different types of road that can be encountered. From open A roads, B roads with restricted view and tighter single-track unclassified roads, they all pose their own individual problems.

It is true that the majority of incidents occur in towns and cities at junctions but the rest can be attributed to the open road. The following are causes of such incidents; running off the road, careless riding, aggressive braking, poor handling skills, poor overtaking skills, excessive speed and loss of control. All risk factors can be reduced through further motorcycle training.

Riders are attracted by the fast flowing twisty corners and the pleasure that rural roads offer but in reality far too many ride at speeds that exceed their actual ability. Riding too fast can also cause car drivers not to judge the rider's speed correctly, this may be when they fail to see when they pull out in front of a speeding motorcycle.

New riders must stay alert, read the road well ahead and be aware of what is happening behind them. A central riding position is good for learner riders. It allows them to dominate their lane and protect their own road space, giving more room for rider error. Riding at a speed that matches rider ability rather than riding at a perceived ability will reduce the dangers for new riders, peer pressure is a huge factor where excessive speed is prevalent.

New riders mostly ride 125cc motorcycles or less. Because of this, they are slower than other traffic, less powerful and can be more vulnerable than other road users. This is evident on faster sections of road where impatient vehicle drivers behind want to pass as soon as possible.

Most rural accidents occur in corners because riders travel faster than their ability. Understanding techniques such as counter steering and reading the road for bend severity are important factors to improving rider skill and safety. Taking further training and education will allow new riders to develop and practice with guidance and coaching, making them more confident and ready for any journey.

MOTORCYCLE
RIDERS HUB

FIRST TIME ON THE ROAD

Having completed the CBT Course, riding independently for the first time can be a daunting prospect. New riders must avoid rushing and should plan short, local journeys to start with to build confidence and experience. They should complete their safety checks and always wear full motorcycle protective clothing for every ride.

From the very first journey, new riders must take responsibility by assuming they won't be seen. Anticipating the actions of other road users is vital and riding defensively within their own ability is the key to success. Regarding motorcycle clothing, give priority to being seen rather than looking fashionable, although there are some great looking brands available now to serve both purposes.

New riders should think before every manoeuvre and develop good all round vision, observations and life-savers. They should take care at road junctions, especially during peak times and reduced visibility, due to weather conditions or heavy traffic.

They should always consider the weather and make sure they have sufficient layers of clothing and waterproofs for wet and cold conditions. If travelling on a long journey, they should also plan regular rest and drink stops along their route, being aware how easily rider fatigue and dehydration can impact their concentration.

It takes time to become comfortable with riding alone especially when wearing a helmet, gloves, jacket and boots for the first time. New riders should be patient with themselves, look out for things that might cause rider distraction. For example, gloves or boots that are brand new and too tight can cause discomfort or pain, they can easily become a distraction and add to a novice rider's risk.

New riders must also take their time to become proficient with their own motorcycle. Getting comfortable with the bikes acceleration and braking characteristics, along with where the controls are and how to use them. Always be aware of the fuel tank capacity and the bikes range to prevent running out of fuel.

KEEP IT ON THE BLACK STUFF

FURTHER TRAINING

In order to ride a motorcycle or moped, all new riders must complete the Compulsory Basic Training (CBT) first. They must also hold a provisional Category 'A' or 'AM' driving licence. By default, a full car driving licence will have the provisional motorcycle entitlement. With a CBT, riders aged 16 can only ride a 50cc moped and riders aged 17 or over can ride a 125cc motorcycle.

Riders must display L plates and cannot carry passengers or ride on motorways. A CBT certificate is only valid for two years, all riders can improve their skills by passing a full motorcycle test. This requires a theory test, further motorcycle training and the two part practical motorcycle test known as the Module 1 and Module 2 tests.

Depending on the riders age, passing this practical test results in the following:

Age 16+ = AM (moped licence)

50cc (restricted to 28mph) moped without L plates. Can carry pillion passengers but cannot use the motorway.

Age 17+ = A1 (light motorbike licence)

125cc without L plates. Can carry pillion passengers and can use the motorway.

Age 19+ = A2 (standard licence)

A bike up to 35Kw (46.6 bhp) without L plates. Can carry pillion passengers and can use the motorway. *Nb. After two years or from age 24, can take Category 'A' motorcycle test to gain unrestricted motorcycle licence. In theory, a Category 'A' unrestricted licence is possible from age 21.*

Age 24+ = A (unrestricted licence)

This is commonly known as the Direct Access Scheme (DAS) test, with training on a motorcycle of 595 cc and at least 50 Kw (54 Bhp). Must be 24 or have held an A2 licence for at least two years (known as Accelerated Access).

KEEP IT ON THE BLACK STUFF

TAKE RESPONSIBILITY

You must accept that to improve your riding skills you must undertake ongoing coaching and guidance. Rarely does your perceived ability match your actual ability but some riders tend to think they are better than they actually are.

The importance of ongoing training is crystal clear to develop performance. The Module 1 and Module 2 tests are mere stepping stones to your riding future. They are to biking what base camp is to Mount Everest, to reach the summit of what is possible on two wheels, requires a willingness and an effort to undertake further training.

Motorcycle training schools can guide you on the best advanced training route. They can advise on the Enhanced Rider Scheme (ERS), which is run by Driver and Vehicle Standards Agency (DVSA) instructors. Advanced rider qualifications can then be taken through organisations such as The Royal Society for the Prevention of Accidents (ROSPA) and the Institute of Advanced Motorists (IAM).

You must always take responsibility for your own riding and actions and always commit to ongoing training and development.

If it is accepted that as a biker, your safety is always in your own hands, you will grow into a proficient rider and be able to **Keep it on the black stuff**.

Printed in Great Britain
by Amazon

37199089R00025